DOGS HELPING PEOPLE

Sheepherding Dogs
Rounding Up the Herd

Alice B. McGinty

The Rosen Publishing Group's
PowerKids Press™
New York

Published in 1999 by The Rosen Publishing Group, Inc.
29 East 21st Street, New York, NY 10010

First Edition

Book Design: Michael de Guzman

Photo Credits: Cover and pp. 12, 15 © Charles Palek/Animals Animals; p. 4 © Fritz Prenzel/Animals Animals; p. 7 © Dennie Cody/FPG International; p. 8 © Paul McCormick/Image Bank; p. 11 © Frans Lemmens/Image Bank; p. 16 © Charles Weckler/Image Bank; p. 19 © Jerry Sieve/FPG International; p. 20 © Robert Pearcy/Animals Animals.

McGinty, Alice B. (Alice Blumenthal)
    Sheep-herding dogs: rounding up the herd /by Alice B. McGinty.
        p.   cm. — (Dogs helping people)
    Includes index.
    Summary: Describes the life of Sparkle, a border collie that works as a sheep dog,
    examining the training and effort involved for sheep-herding dogs to do their job.
    ISBN 0-8239-5219-3
    1. Sheep dogs—Juvenile literature. 2. Border collie—Juvenile literature. [1. Sheep dogs 2. Border collie. 3. Dogs.] I. Title. II. Series.
    SF428.6.M34 1998
    636.737—dc21   97-52011
                                                     CIP
                                                     AC

Manufactured in the United States of America

Contents

Sparkle

Sparkle is a Border collie puppy. She is black and white and full of energy. She is also very smart. Sparkle's favorite person is Kay. Sparkle and Kay live on a farm. Every day Sparkle follows Kay around the farm while she works.

There is always lots of work to do on a farm. When Sparkle gets bigger, she will help with the work. Sparkle is going to be a sheepherding dog, just like her mother and many of her **ancestors** (AN-ses-terz).

◁ It's hard to imagine these cuddly Border collie puppies herding sheep. But someday they will!

Raising Sheep

Since **ancient** (AYN-shent) times, people have raised sheep for wool and meat. **Shepherds** (SHEH-perdz) watch over the sheep on a farm and move them around to **graze** (GRAYZ). Shepherds use sheepherding dogs to keep together their groups of sheep, or **flocks** (FLOKS), and to move them from place to place.

But how does one small dog move a flock of sheep? The sheepherding dog acts like a **predator** (PREH-duh-ter). The way he moves shows that he's the boss. When the dog comes near, the sheep move the other way.

A shepherd and his sheepherding dog work together as a team to move the ▷ sheep where they're supposed to go.

6

Herding

One day, Kay lets Sparkle play in the farmyard. Sparkle sees some ducks. Sparkle runs in circles around the ducks. The ducks huddle together. Then Sparkle walks toward the ducks, forcing them to move closer to Kay. "Oh, Sparkle," laughs Kay. "You herd sheep, not ducks!" Gathering animals and making them move is called **herding** (HUR-ding). Sheepherding **breeds** (BREEDZ) are born with an **instinct** (IN-stinkt) to herd. They have been herding sheep for hundreds of years and are born knowing how to do it.

◁ *Driving, or moving the sheep from one place to another, is just one of a sheepherding dog's jobs.*

Training

A Border collie already has the instinct to herd. But to be a good sheepherder, the dog needs training. Every dog in training must learn to take the sheep where her master wants them. She also must learn not to hurt the sheep while herding them.

A trainer will teach the dog some simple commands, such as "Come," "Down," and "Stay." Many dogs, like Sparkle, are trained by their owners. Other dogs are taken to special trainers.

The trainers and shepherds who work with their sheepherding dogs respect ▷ them for their hard work.

Herding Commands

A **handler** (HAND-ler) owns a dog and also works with it during training. "Come by," the handler commands, moving in a circle around the sheep. The dog follows. Her instinct is to keep the sheep between her and the handler. "Way to me," the handler commands, and he circles around the sheep in the other direction. The dog follows. "Walk up," the handler commands now.

A sheepherding dog will always stay a certain ▷ distance from the sheep.

The dog runs toward the sheep, making them move. "Take time!" the handler says. This means the dog should slow down and not move too close to the sheep.

Advanced Training

The dog has learned to bring in sheep from far away. Now she's ready to learn harder skills. One skill is called **driving** (DRY-ving). Driving is moving sheep away from the handler. This takes practice, because the dog's instinct is to move sheep toward the handler.

Shedding (SHEH-ding) is separating one or more sheep from the flock. Since sheep like to stay together, this can be hard to do. Shedding is used to separate sheep who need medicine. It's also used to remove strays from the flock.

Sheep who are separated from the flock are quickly returned so they are not attacked by predators like wolves. ▷

Dog at Work

Now the dog and her master are working on the farm. It's **shearing** (SHEER-ing) time for the sheep. "Come by," the master commands. The dog dashes off, circling around the sheep. "Walk up," he calls. The dog moves the sheep toward her master. He opens the gate. With his shepherd's **crook** (KRUHK), the handler guides the sheep into the pen.

One sheep won't go in. The dog crouches down and stares at the sheep. This is called "the eye." The sheep thinks the dog might attack. So the sheep goes into the pen.

◁ *Giving a sheep "the eye" reminds it that the dog is in charge.*

Sheepdog Trials

Sheepherding dogs and their handlers work hard to become good at what they do. Sheepdog contests, or **trials** (TRYLZ), give them a chance to show off.

At a sheepdog trial, a handler commands his dog to fetch five sheep from 400 yards away. The dog drives the sheep around turns and through gates. Then the dog and handler shed two sheep and put them all into a pen.

The dog and handler who complete the course with the fastest time and the fewest mistakes win.

The close teamwork between a handler and his dog can be ▷ seen at sheepdog trials.

(18)

Guard Dogs

The sheepdog and her handler are at a sheepdog trial. Is the handler worried about his sheep who are alone at the farm? No. The handler knows the sheep are safe. Two guard dogs are watching them. A guard dog is another type of dog that works on a farm. The handler's guard dogs have lived with the sheep all their lives. Guard dogs are **independent** (in-dee-PEN-dent), strong, and very loyal to the sheep. They stay with the sheep all the time. And they protect them from predators, such as coyotes or wolves.

◁ *With its white coat and long, shaggy hair, a komondor blends in with his flock of sheep. This helps him protect the flock.*

People and Dogs, Working Together

Like Sparkle, sheepherding dogs are eager to do their jobs. Other working dogs, such as herding dogs and guard dogs, help with cattle, hogs, and goats too. They are all smart, full of energy, and ready to work.

It would take many shepherds to do the work of one sheepherding dog and its handler. A dog's speed and herding instinct, along with the handler's control, make quite a team!

Glossary

ancestor (AN-ses-ter) A relative who lived before you.

ancient (AYN-shent) From a long time ago.

breed (BREED) A group of animals that look very much alike and have the same ancestors.

crook (KRUHK) A stick with a curved end that shepherds use to herd sheep.

driving (DRY-ving) Moving sheep in a direction away from the handler.

graze (GRAYZ) To feed on grass.

flock (FLOK) A group of the same kind of animals.

handler (HAND-ler) The owner of a dog, such as a farmer or shepherd, who also trains the dog.

herding (HUR-ding) Gathering animals and making them move.

independent (in-dee-PEN-dent) Being able to do things without help.

instinct (IN-stinkt) An urge to act a certain way.

predator (PREH-duh-ter) An animal that hunts and kills other animals for food.

shearing (SHEER-ing) Shaving the wool off a sheep.

shedding (SHEH-ding) Separating one or more sheep from the flock.

shepherd (SHEH-perd) The person who cares for and herds sheep.

trial (TRYL) A contest.

Index